How to Be a
Big
Kid

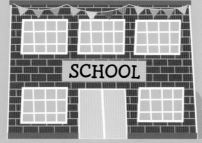

SCHOOL

DK | Penguin Random House

Editor Hélène Hilton
Design and Illustration Charlotte Bull
US Editor Mindy Fichter
US Senior Editor Shannon Beatty
Editorial Assistance Violet Peto
Additional Design and Illustration Rachael Hare
Producer, Pre-Production Dragana Puvacic
Producer John Casey
Educational Consultant Penny Coltman
Jacket Designer Charlotte Bull
Jacket Coordinator Francesca Young
Managing Editor Penny Smith
Managing Art Editor Mabel Chan
Publisher Mary Ling
Art Director Jane Bull

First American Edition, 2018
Published in the United States by DK Publishing
345 Hudson Street, New York, New York 10014

Copyright © 2018 Dorling Kindersley Limited
DK, a Division of Penguin Random House LLC
10 9 8 7 6 5 4 3 2
002–307863–May/2018

A catalog record for this book
is available from the Library of Congress.
ISBN 978-1-4654-6858-1

DK books are available at special discounts when purchased in bulk
for sales promotions, premiums, fund-raising, or educational use.
For details, contact: DK Publishing Special Markets,
345 Hudson Street, New York, New York 10014
SpecialSales@dk.com

Printed and bound in China

A WORLD OF IDEAS:
SEE ALL THERE IS TO KNOW

www.dk.com

Contents

4   All about you!

6   Who's in your family?

8   How do you feel today?

10   Very important manners

12   Underpants go first

14   What will you wear today?

16   Squeaky clean

18   Sparkly teeth

20   Potty time

22   Your first sleepover

24   Your amazing body

26   Happy heart

28   Look at all this food!

30   You and the universe

32   Take care of our planet

34   Very important living things

36   Stay safe

38   Sing and sign

40   Sing and learn

42   How to be a really good friend

44   Look at what I can do!

46   Hello, school!

48   Index

All about you!

From the color of your eyes to the shape of your nose, you are one of a kind from the day you are born. And every day since then, you've become even more special.

No one in the whole world looks like you. We all have different faces and bodies, as well as different hair, eye, and skin colors.

You are completely unique, totally special, and perfectly you.

No matter how you look, you are perfect just as you are.

All the things that you like, from your favorite toys to the friends and family you love, also make you who you are.

The choices you make are also a part of you. Being kind and friendly are choices that you make every day. What will you choose today?

Here are some ways you can practice.

Your name is who you are!

Practice writing the letters in your name to learn how to spell it.

With a pen or pencil on paper

In the air with your finger

In a steamed-up mirror or window

With a stick in the sand

With pebbles

With modeling clay

Who's in your family?

Your family is made up of the people who take care of you, make you feel safe, and love you no matter what.

Hello! I live with my mom and dad.

Hey! I have a mom, a dad, two sisters, and three brothers.

Hi! I was adopted by my mom and dad.

Hi! My sisters and I have two dads who take care of us.

Each family is **different** and **special**.

Hello! My mom takes care of my brother and me.

Hey! I live with my mom, my stepdad, and stepbrother.

New siblings

Is there a new baby in your family?

Congratulations!

Here are some things you can do together to be friends.

Cuddle the baby.

Play with the baby.

Read to the baby.

Talk to the baby.

Babies cry because they can't talk yet, but babies can understand words before they can speak. Chat to your baby to help them learn faster.

How do you feel today?

Emotions are important because they tell you how you feel. All your feelings are worth listening to.

happy

excited

Face game

Can you guess how the people around you are feeling today? **How can you tell?**

tired

scared

calm

I'm all shy!

If you feel shy, sometimes words just don't want to come out. That's okay, you just need to take a deep breath. You will get more confident with some practice.

nervous

angry

If I get very upset, my emotions want to come out all at once! I take a breath to calm down and use my words to say how I feel.

lonely

Look at all these emotions. Can you think of things that make you feel like this?

sad

grumpy

embarrassed

What are tears?

Tears are drops of salty water that come from a pouch near the eye. People cry when they are sad or hurt, but also if they are happy and laughing. Weird!

9

Hello!
It's nice
to meet you.

Saying "hello" is a nice way to greet someone.

Very important manners

Being **polite** shows others that you **care** about their feelings. Your best manners make people **smile!**

Ask nicely
by saying
"please."

Please
can you help me?

Thank you
for my present!
I love it!

Saying **"thank you"** shows that you are grateful.

If you need to interrupt someone or get their attention, say **"excuse me."**

Excuse me!
This is really important.

Bye!
See you later!

Don't forget to say **"good-bye"** when you leave.

I am really, really
sorry
I hurt your feelings.

Apologizing shows that you know you were wrong and won't do it again.

Nervous giggles
Lots of children giggle when they are yelled at because they feel embarrassed. If this happens to you, try to stay calm and listen so that you can learn.

Put your **legs** in the two small holes of your **underpants**.

Socks go on your feet.

Underpants
go first
Useful things to know when you get dressed.

Do **gloves** go on your **ears**?

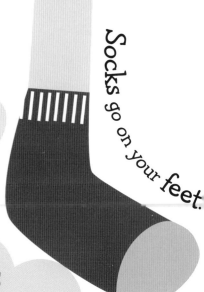

No! Gloves go on your **hands**!

Left

Right

Shoes go on this way.

Put your feet here!

Shoelaces can be tricky when you start off, so ask someone to show you how to do it. If you practice a lot you'll be doing your own laces very soon!

Zipper or buttons?

Most buttons are done up by putting the button through the **buttonhole.**

Zippers are made up of little teeth that come together to close. Pull the zipper up to bring the teeth together.

Check the label so you put your shirt the right way around. The label goes in the back.

Try laying out your clothes on the floor before putting them on to make sure they're not inside out.

What will you wear today?

Pick the perfect clothes for you to wear today.

Spring

In **spring**, there are showers and rainbows. **Can you find a raincoat, rain boots, an umbrella, and a rain hat?**

Summer

In **summer**, the weather is sunny and hot. **Can you find a sun hat, sunglasses, shorts, a T-shirt, and sandals?**

Fall

In **fall**, the weather is cool and windy.

Can you find a sweater, a scarf, pants, and shoes?

Winter

In **winter**, it's cold and it sometimes snows.

Can you find snow boots, a coat, a knitted hat, and gloves?

15

Squeaky clean
from head to toe

Here's a little guide to making sure you always feel (and smell) as fresh as a daisy.

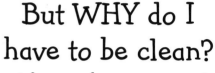

Germs are tiny little things that can make you feel **sick**.

But WHY do I have to be clean?

Apart from making sure you don't become all smelly and itchy, being clean helps to keep germs away.

Tissues ready!

Blow your nose by closing your mouth and blowing as hard as you can, out of your nostrils into a tissue.

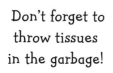

Don't forget to throw tissues in the garbage!

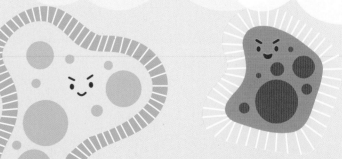

Catch those germs!

Cover your mouth when you cough to stop germs from spreading to other people. Then wash your hands.

Wash your hands!

Keep your hands germ-free by washing them well with soap and water, especially before eating.

Take care of your nails

Your nails keep growing all the time. Have them clipped to keep them short and tidy.

Shower time

Take a shower or a bath to wash yourself with soap and water. Make shower time more fun by singing as loudly as you can!

Brush your hair

Brush or comb your hair to keep it from getting tangled.

Shampoo makes your hair shiny and clean. Keep your eyes closed!

Sparkly teeth

Your teeth need you to take care of them so they stay **healthy** and sparkling. Brush them **twice a day** for **two whole minutes**.

I'm a front tooth: an **incisor**. My sharp edge cuts food.

I'm a side tooth: a **canine**. I am pointy to tear food.

Dentists are special teeth doctors. They check and clean your teeth to make sure they are healthy.

I'm a big back tooth: a **molar**. I mash food into tiny bits.

Wobbly tooth

When you're ready for grown-up teeth, your baby teeth become wobbly and fall out. This makes space for your big teeth!

But WHY should I brush my teeth?

Brushing helps to protect your teeth against germs that make little holes (cavities) in your teeth.

Sugary things like soda pop and candy can also damage your teeth.

How to brush your teeth
(and do a really, really good job)

1 Squeeze a little blob of toothpaste onto your toothbrush.

2 Move your brush up and down over your teeth.

3 Keep brushing for two minutes, making sure you brush the front, back, and underneath parts of your teeth.

4 Spit out the toothpaste and rinse your toothbrush.

5 All done! Your teeth are sparkly clean and minty fresh.

Get a grown-up to help you floss, which helps to clean between your teeth!

Potty time

If it's time to be out of diapers,
it's time to learn what to do
with a grown-up toilet.

If you need the
bathroom, don't wait
until it's an emergency.

Bathrooms outside of
houses, like at school
or in restaurants, can be
different from the bathrooms
you have at home. If you feel
unsure about them, check
with a grown-up.

1 Sit on the toilet.

2 Do your business.

3 Wipe from front to back
with toilet paper until
you're all clean.

4 Flush!

5 Wash your hands.

Carefully, with
soap and water.
(EVERY TIME!)

20

If you do have an accident, ask a grown-up to help you get clean and dry.

Everyone has little accidents from time to time, especially when you are first out of diapers. Try not to worry!

Try to always go to the bathroom right before bedtime.

Nighttime accidents

If you have an accident while you sleep, it's not your fault. Lots of children wet the bed, so don't be embarrassed. Bed-wetting goes away all on its own after a while.

21

Your first sleepover

Sleepovers are so much fun! Whose house are you sleeping at tonight?

Don't forget your favorite cuddly toy.

Follow the swirly line to get ready for bed.

All tucked in

Say good night

Lights out!

Spooky dark

Not being able to see what's around you can be scary. But if you can't have a night-light, remind yourself that you are safe in your bed.

Put your pajamas on

Brush your teeth

Bedtime story

Go to the bathroom

Sweet dreams

I love sleepovers at my grandparents' house. I always get a bedtime story.

Your amazing body

From the top of your head to the tips of your toes, your body is perfect.

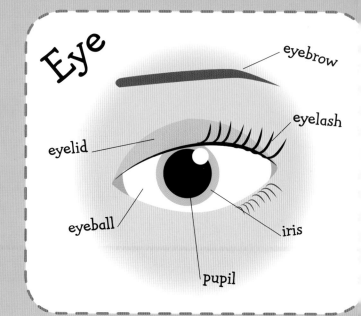

Eye

- eyebrow
- eyelash
- eyelid
- eyeball
- iris
- pupil

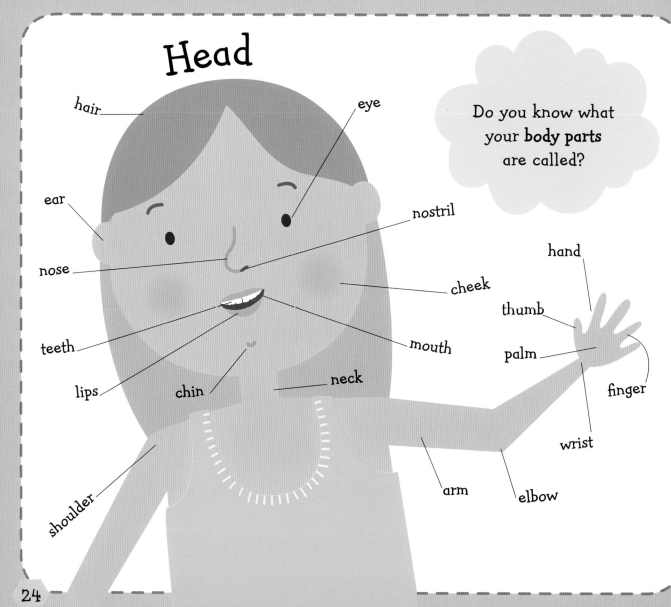

Head

- hair
- eye
- ear
- nostril
- nose
- cheek
- teeth
- mouth
- lips
- chin
- neck
- shoulder
- arm
- elbow
- hand
- thumb
- palm
- finger
- wrist

Do you know what your **body parts** are called?

Body

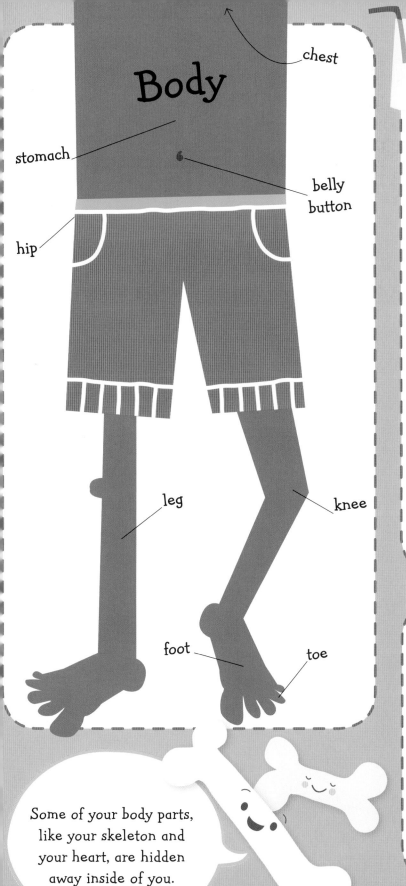

chest

stomach

belly button

hip

leg

knee

foot

toe

Some of your body parts, like your skeleton and your heart, are hidden away inside of you.

Eat well

Your body needs you to eat different types of food to stay strong and healthy. Here are some things you should eat every day:

Lots of **fruit** and **vegetables**.

Some starchy food, like **bread** or **rice**.

Some protein, such as **meat**, **eggs**, or **beans**.

Some healthy oil, like **avocados** or **nuts**.

Move your body

You are meant to move, run, jump, dance, and use lots of energy. Your body needs to exercise to stay strong.

Happy heart

Feeling happy is one of the
best things in the world!

What makes you happy?

being read to

cuddly
toys

hugs

painting

Sleepy time

Your body and your mind
need sleep to feel ready for
a new day. Children need
to sleep for around 10
or 11 hours every night.

family

pets

making friends

Draw a picture of all the things that make you happy. Think about the people who make you smile and the things you love doing.

playing

sports

No one can be happy all the time. The best you can do is to keep trying to be happy as often as you can!

Look at all this food!

There is so much food to try and taste. Which of these are your favorites?

tomatoes

noodles

zucchini

beets

broccoli

cauliflower

carrot

chili

corn

peas

potato

sweet potato

bread

rice

orange

strawberries

grapes

pineapple

olive oil

apple

watermelon

blackberries

kiwi

fish

honey

meat

milk

eggs

All the food that we eat either comes from a plant or an animal.

You and the universe

Our planet, Earth, is just one tiny little planet in the whole big wide universe!

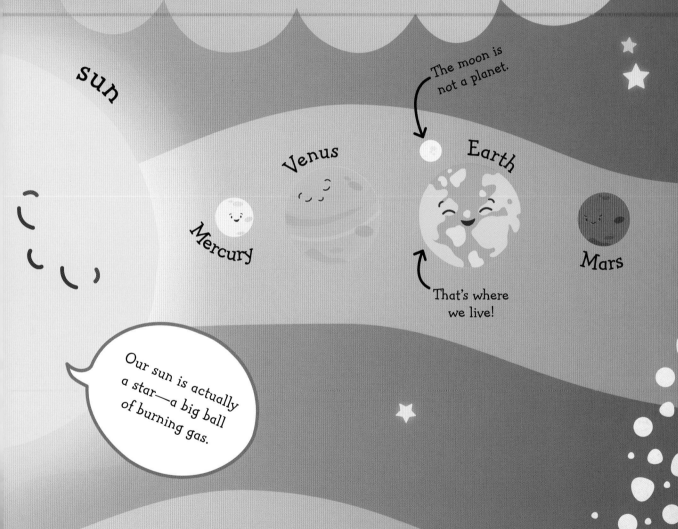

sun

The moon is not a planet.

Earth

Venus

Mercury

That's where we live!

Mars

Our sun is actually a star—a big ball of burning gas.

Look at the sky at night to see far away stars and planets. No one knows how big the universe is. It might go on forever and ever.

The universe is EVERYTHING. It's all of time and space and everything in it.

Sometimes you can spot Mars and other planets in the sky at night. They look tiny because they're so far away.

Saturn

Neptune

Uranus

Jupiter

Earth is the only planet we know of in the whole universe that has living things (like you) on it.

Our solar system

Earth is one of eight planets that spin around the sun. Together they make up the solar system.

Take care
of our planet

Our planet, Earth, takes care of us by giving us food, water, and energy. But we also need to take care of the Earth before it becomes too damaged.

You can help save our planet.

Paper, cardboard, glass, some metals, and some plastics can be recycled.

That means they can be reused instead of just being garbage! Isn't that great?

Grow some of your own food or buy food that was grown close to home.

Turn lights off to save energy.

Make your yard friendly to little animals that might need to live there.

What can you do to help?

Plant a tree. Trees make the air cleaner.

Recycle your trash.

Walk or bike rather than drive to save fuel.

Very important living things

There are so many different animals and plants in the world that we still haven't discovered all of them. Which of these do you already know?

hippopotamus

snake

bee

dog

pigeon

butterfly

worm

chicken

polar bear

cat

sunflower

seed

shark

duck

Plants and animals are things that are alive.

flower

crab

rabbit

leaves

snail

ants

tiger

elephant

tree

dragonfly

horse

goldfish

human

frog

Living things need to be cared for. Animals can't talk, but they can feel pain, *so* it's important to be nice to them.

Stay safe

You are a very special person, so learn to keep yourself safe and sound.

Be careful around water.

To **cross the road**, hold a grown-up's hand, use a pedestrian crossing, and check both ways for cars.

Watch out for cars!

Don't touch electricity.

Wear a **seat belt** when you're in the car.

Hello!

Never speak to **someone you don't know on the Internet or in real life** without checking with a grown-up first.

Your body belongs to you.

No one should ever touch or make you do anything with your body that you don't want to do.

Don't **keep secrets** that make you sad or worried.

If you see anything on a **computer, phone, or tablet** that upsets you, walk away and go and tell you a grown-up.

!

Don't play near railroad tracks.

What number should you call in an emergency?

1 2 3
4 5 6
7 8 9
0

Always talk to someone you trust if you are feeling sad or worried.

Here are some people you can talk to:

someone in your family you trust
a police officer
a doctor
a nurse
someone at daycare or school

Sing and sign

Here are some fun songs you can
sing and act out with your hands.

The itsy bitsy spider climbed up the waterspout.

Down came the rain and washed the spider out.

Out came the sun and dried up all the rain,

And the itsy bitsy spider climbed up the spout again.

I'm a little teapot, short and stout.

Here is my handle; here is my spout.

When I get all steamed up hear me shout.

Tip me over and pour me out.

This little piggy went to market.

This little piggy stayed at home.

This little piggy had roast beef.

This little piggy had none.

And this little piggy went...

"Wee, wee, wee," all the way home.

If you're happy and you know it, clap your hands.

If you're happy and you know it, clap your hands.

If you're happy and you know it,

and you really want to show it,

If you're happy and you know it,

clap your hands!

Sing and learn

Learn some super-useful things while you sing your little heart out!

You can sing the "Alphabet Song" to the tune of "Twinkle, Twinkle, Little Star."

"Alphabet Song"

A B C D E F G

H I J K L M N O P

Q R S T U and V

W X Y and Z.

Now I know my ABC's,

Next time won't you sing with me?

The "Alphabet Song" teaches you the names of all the letters. Do you know what sound the letters make when they are in words?

Fish and count to ten

One, two, three, four, five.

Once I caught a fish alive.

Six, seven, eight, nine, ten.

Then I let it go again.

Why did you let it go?

Because it bit my finger so.

Which finger did it bite?

This little finger on my right!

How to be a really good friend

Friends are so much fun! Here are some tips to make a lot of new friends.

If someone looks sad or lonely, ask them if they want to play.

Share your toys or treats with others. Then maybe they will share with you, too.

Playing nicely means being kind to each other.

NO!

If you've upset someone, try to understand what you have done wrong, and say you're "sorry."

If someone is being mean to you or to someone else, say "NO!," tell them how they are making you feel, and let a grown-up know right away.

Take turns so that you each can play. Be fair!

What's a bully?

Bullies pick on others. Often bullies are people who don't know how to make friends, so they act mean to feel included. If someone is bullying, you should tell a grown-up, but you could also show the bully how to be kind and play nicely.

43

Look at what I can do!

Here is a whole bunch of **awesome** stuff you can try, too. **You can do it!**

- ☐ Ride a bike or scooter
- ☐ Swim with water wings
- ☐ Make an obstacle course
- ☐ Climb a tree (carefully)
- ☐ Build a nature den
- ☐ Make mud art
- ☐ Play catch
- ☐ Go on a color hunt

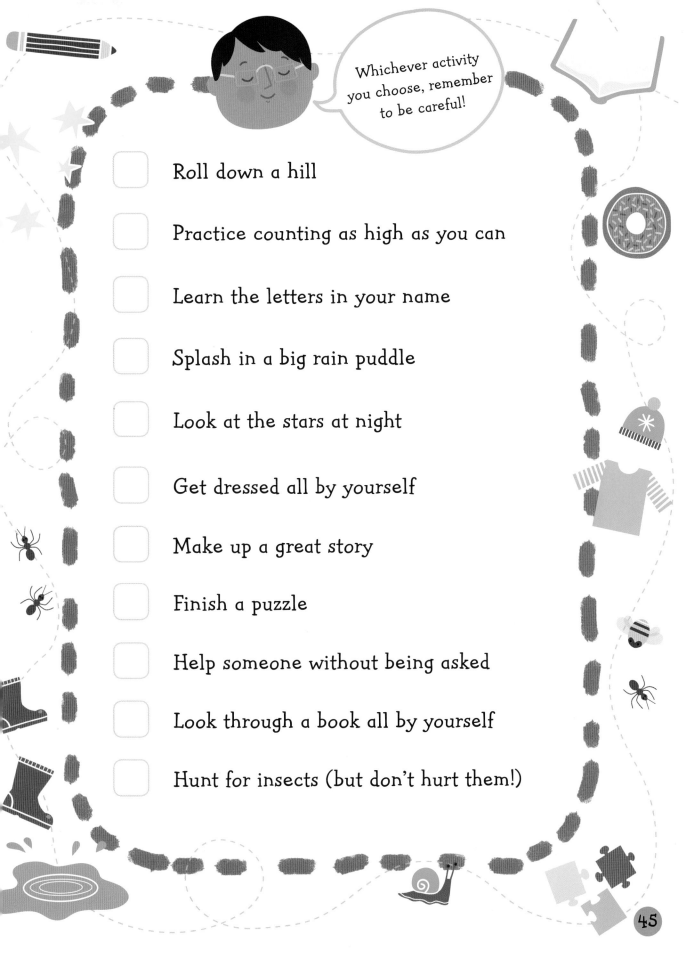

Whichever activity you choose, remember to be careful!

- [ ] Roll down a hill
- [ ] Practice counting as high as you can
- [ ] Learn the letters in your name
- [ ] Splash in a big rain puddle
- [ ] Look at the stars at night
- [ ] Get dressed all by yourself
- [ ] Make up a great story
- [ ] Finish a puzzle
- [ ] Help someone without being asked
- [ ] Look through a book all by yourself
- [ ] Hunt for insects (but don't hurt them!)

Hello, school!

It's your first day of school! There are so many new things to say "hello" to.

SCHOOL

Hello, **playground**

Hello, **classroom**

Hello, **coatrack**

Hello, **friends**

Hello, **principal**

Hello, **teacher**

Hello, **toys**

Say "see you later" to Mom and Dad. They'll be back after school.

Index

A
Accidents 21
Alphabet 40
Animals 29, 33,
    34-35, 38-39

B
Baby 7
Bedtime 21, 22-23
Body 24-25, 26, 37
Bully 43

C
Clean 16-17, 18, 19
Clothes 13, 14-15
Counting 41, 45

E
Earth 30-31, 32-33
Emotions 8-9
Exercise 25

F
Family 5, 6-7, 27
Food 18, 25, 28-29,
    33
Friends 5, 7, 27,
    42-43, 47

G
Germs 16

H
Heart 25, 26

I
Internet 36

L
Left and right 12
Letters 5, 40, 45

M
Manners 10-11

P
Pets 27
Planet 30-31, 32-33
Plants 29, 34, 35
Playing 27, 42

R
Recycling 32-33

S
Safety 36-37
School 20, 46-47
Seasons 14-15
Shoelaces 13
Sleep 21, 22-23, 26
Song 38-39, 40-41
Stars 30, 45

T
Teeth 18-19, 23, 24
Toilet 20-21, 23

U
Universe 30-31

Acknowledgments

The publisher would like to thank the following for
their kind permission to reproduce their photographs:

(Key: a-above; b-below/bottom; c-center; f-far; l-left; r-right; t-top)

28 Dreamstime.com: Leszek Ogrodnik / Lehu (c, cr); Tracy Decourcy / Rimglow (c/Carrot); Pichest
Boonpanchua / Khumthong (br). **29 Dreamstime.com:** Leszek Ogrodnik / Lehu (ca). Getty Images:
Burazin / Photographer's Choice RF (cra). **34 123RF.com:** Eric Isselee / isselee (crb/Polar bear cub);
Ievgen Kovalev / genjok (cb). **Dreamstime.com:** Irochka (cb/Sunflower); Isselee (crb). **Fotolia:** Eric
Isselee (cl). **35 Dreamstime.com:** Liligraphie (cl); Natalya Aksenova (tc). **iStockphoto.com:** Taalvi (crb)

All other images © Dorling Kindersley
For further information see: www.dkimages.com